AF478694

THE
JUKEBOX
OF
MEMNON

Also by Ray DiPalma

Max (1969)
Macaroons [with Stephen Shrader] (1969)
Between the Shapes (1970)
The Gallery Goers (1971)
All Bowed Down (1972)
Works in a Drawer (1972)
Borgia Circles (1972)
Time Being [with Asa Benveniste & Tom Raworth] (1972)
Soli (1974)
The Sargasso Transcries (1974)
Max / A Sequel (1974)
Accidental Interludes (1975)
Marquee (1977)
Cuiva Sails (1978)
Planh (1979)
Observatory Gardens (1979)
Genesis (1980)
Legend [with Bruce Andrews, Charles Bernstein,
  Steve McCaffery & Ron Silliman] (1980)
Labyrinth Radio (1981)
23 Works (1982)
13 Works (1982)
Two Poems (1982)
Chan (1984)
January Zero (1984)
Startle Luna (1984)

THE JUKEBOX OF MEMNON

RAY DI PALMA

Potes & Poets Press Inc. Elmwood, Connecticut. 1988

Acknowledgements

Thanks to the editors of *Ironwood* and *New American Writing* where some of these works originally appeared.

Cover design by Elizabeth DiPalma

ISBN 0–937013–24–2

THE JUKEBOX OF MEMNON

Smoke shave and smoke
another phase in the crowd
tin pan tied to the ear

a soundtrack for a temperament
and bare ass bold at the red piano
you're a sky-colored blunder
we keep around for the gist of the drift

power ends in the versatile
but there's lots of interesting things
pinching in the ravine
where the crickets chirp
and dry needle hoodoo dazzles the cramped

I omit what shames me
and reflects an arch credulity
I would not have you think
this so by phrase and juncture
the salted is jagged into place
intervals to distract and menace
the spread function consuming the accustomed
what is accused to me
softened and sharpened
the hand part the fund of apprehensions
wagers in disarray the enactment of measure
a rampart

Musing
stupefied by indiscretions
and the luminous attitudes
of sleep on the run
my purpose takes on the hubba-hubba
idolatry of the distant and clear
some inflected portion
the once submerged ictus
now painted red or yellow
accumulating its grace out of
the distorted silence and
unresolved wariness that thought made balance

The flaw absorbed in the haphazard
footsteps and pale machinery of sleep
cuts a soft rough edge
dissipated intuition points the way
pausing over a sketch of the extraneous
invisible hours in a dark cellar
a bowl of red and yellow roses
on a large glass table

Craving infinity I succumb
to a virtuosic drowsiness
dividing the exhausted logic
into sudden experiences and
new combinations of the typical
and situate

whistling at the moon with
a mouth full of crackers

Radical words half whispered
half radical half whisper

Quadratics cut the iron of approval
only my eye makes these shapes
bodily decoded

The residue of gumption is structure

                      Calculations
of solace
            as primitive as names

Stopped in the heat
we watched the functionary trim
his truest helmet—a brown paper bag
squared and cuffed into a brimless mitred
capacity

Meaning's mendicant
cuts his way
to a superior murmur
elbowing an exegesis
naked in the imbecile thicket of sleep

the heraldic adjective
fills the essential hours
unconsoled, warm, and rowdy
a little less than music
a little more than mud

an invigorated mercy
abstracts the shaft of sunlight
making a shadow of the orange-haired man
as he sits before his plate of bacon and eggs
too fulfilled in his obscurity to be composed

the luminous fluency of the nail through wood
kin to the blue hammer
essential to the simmering light
and empty arpeggios
brooding in the mist

Like a man whose
white shadow burns a hole
through the window
                    I put
down the soot du jour
one tenth moonlight
nine tenths gypsy words

Painted soapstone
for jade
word after word for travel

Snow
on the tooth
mud
in your eye

Word hoard
philophosphorexcrescent

The line's a rope
across a big door
the wind rattles

Let me show
you a little
about myself
Here's an
aerial view

Metal phantoms slump
in the blue shadow
of the smokestack

a counting nerve buzzes
on the cheek

the fragile generosity
of the bewildered
whispers a bubble
and calls it the moon

Rest obliges the gloom
arching it's back over
sympathy's incoherent buttress
leisure's a rumour
husbanding the matt black
up your head

Mongrel grip and ride
water from the thorn
in good supply
                    sap's
allure culls a dazed
pace
         pebble-grazing

Suspicion
offers a mild exhilaration
so what's next
a savage discussion
of the truth maybe
a line of feeble-minded dents
slowly filling-up with
a variety of sour breath
and affable echoes

Regret peeves the siren ethic
makes the common
a little more local
opportunity knots
the incandescent plethora
an innocuous enthusiasm
uncomplicated by the informed prejudice

A sobering token
like memory
a hunk of marble
veined with momentum
and the subtle oxygen
of scarcity
               good dust
on the intelligent wound

The shrewd pace
of the navigating bird
gravity's ache accumulating
in a cabbage rose
sex in a broken chair
give the chapter
an uncertain vigor
a perverse affirmation
mixes the wary with
the arithmetic of pleasure
take it or leave it
quality means the hands

Mercury mumble it's
a hunch less the vanity
Mercury mumble
it say nimble and numb
enough report
isolate the what
for what the heard
and overheard
much ado about
noting Will's way
to have truck
with the simple
come and go of it
mercury mumble
it stay nimble
knot hobbled
and aligned

Accurate beam got
whose is who's
but whose hoot got
whose accurate beam
who, hmmm?
China Click
Milky Way
Chicago Theory
Radke Blonde
Konzert Explo
accurate beam got
who's who
but whose hoot got
whose accurate beam
who, whom?
Pale Wanda
Viv Vimm
Subtle Penge
Holden Hinge
Rhonda Rose
accurate beam got
whose who
but who's who
hoot hoot hooty hoo
anyway

The scenario stretched out on the stiff dollar
What the episodic makes seem intimate
California canoes full of moonlit health
The immoderate lure of the strictly logical
High wind across the skylight
Slow revolve in the chambered cleft
Circumstance and the tight white word
Through the music of true focus
Engine of the metropolis run on an aspirin
Neon man behind the wheel
Instinctive response to angular momentum

The pressure of lost variance
Cut within the line and frame
Disappointed laughter
Mistakes of silence
Mend the stratagem put wrong
By the transparent glow of decay
Too tender to be resolute
The tolerant humdrum
Smoothed with the hard corn
Of precedent and conviction

either least thought
together
heartens content
obtrudes
together

callous
cosmos
littered with
mule thoughts
tugs in the mix
hearten
put ears
on the peculiar

hard ache
in the squat
of the skeptical
litmus of the satis
errata in totem

kicks the mule
in perfect
silence
knees first
brought up to chin
teeth rattle
under the ceremony
upper lip sweats
blue mule
in perfect silence
nose cuts
a horizon

sea-colored
and taller
in the prolific dark

were you that man
or woman or were
you the predicate

arc-ing in the sun
a comet and scowl
penetrating the syllable's ear

sea-colored
the grey matinee
camera's beam a harvest line

what we know
we hear
in the tumult

written on the window
out of the ice
vacant and green

the arrogant
hold their red knees
in their golden arms

a crystal gong
chides the phantom aptitude
under the wool

put in
or put out
put off
or put on
X marks
the spot
tango
leopard

touchpaper
tactic
icon code
won one
in the dark
no mercy notes
signal a
map of smiles

that's it
that's the
way it's
going to
be that's
the way it's
got its yes
got it, yes

my politics
step on the eye
step on the ear
stepping out
yes for got it
yes for the stick
that touches
the first one

reed
or ready
word

Interpretations
sleep on the dial
reinventing the margins
between us erasing
the hardness and replacing
it with the conclusive conditional
pure tense
where the echo spills

Storms cool the flares
shadowblown grackles and ravens
double and glare and scoff

starlight fixes the bait
mallet against a cool rim of steel
denial accomodates an improvised verdict

all digressive subterfuge
trivial motive and morbid parallel
churn and drudge in the argument

unmusical but an aurora's dynamics
intercepted patching the violent and elusive
parade in the pagan battered warp

shock intervenes the rhymes
red bright on grey
the washed thought

mercury doors
a specific fathom
grasped that is

or what is hidden
in measure
a specific fathom

time of day from
here to there
and back again

inside the sides
a wink to fuse
the thought watched

rumour's rooster
halloos the distorted
strata of analogies

my A is a vegetable A
my Z is a vegetable A
profligate and tangential

is the balance
commercial and run by
the transmission of

the undeclared
or the strange low
coherences of the ear

when and where there
is no such thing
the thought walked

household bones

and a rainbow

in the lungs

subtract a coyote

and a few rusty hinges

and the fossil records

say poems

Not
thought
the store
but the notion
led
the motionless
exchange
disrupted
sets the pattern
of memory
history distorts
desire
deformity
unchanged
continuing instead

The view from Professor Logick's overlook

Dedication's meal spread on the flood

A wall or
agent pattern

Attention
turned perfection

Black plateaus
Red lion
Drunk mask
Facing the sunset
Something something
Shells and apes

Thinking
along
words

Under the red swimmer

Systemic reprisal of the active eye

A lane

Hardlight on a list

Hardlit code

Obedience
to the lie
and the land

To work the mouth

to repeat the sovereignty

of distance

The isolated goal

protected by the empty

trajectory

Heard twice:

one . . . two

hey . . . you

one . . . two

Thus calibrated

the honor touches

back . . . for more

than memory's sake

             Into these
one example
for example
          one of these

          Artifice tapering
and charged

          Controlled
for instance
          by the logic
   that closes
   into these

One other example
for example
one of these

          A papery face
          put on
          for logic

An afterthought
heavy as a saint
holds my coat
(my full orchestration)

The brick ship
has a grace
capsized
It does that

It's a distracted fitness
reckoned but
undeduced . . . congruent
with the justly momentary
not in a legible spectrum
but a prevision
no, rather a
proviso of climate
where you wait and see
or where as the saying goes
you wait and see
not captive buy amply
provided for by the anticipation
that keeps you afloat

Each moment is surrounded
by the correct torrent

    Each moment is
    surrounded by
    the correct torment

The sphere's endless erasures
and a longer calm protect the song

A full moon
makes a litigant of the tides
Their issue
they'd have you know
is the province of apprehension
where the joke clatters through eloquence
and its busy simplicity to postpone the marvelous

Embracing yet another version
of the sham paragon you heave majestically
in the thickening denials
There is much to be answered for
based on a play by one so big
his name need not be mentioned

And how much longer
can you continue to spit in the face
of the baggy scholar gentry
for they are many and their sincerities
come like the loaves and fishes

on page 9 we find
the lost world
and send back word
of the expedition
the unknown
is jettisoned in favor
of a pile of
pineapple paper and
a large desk

what the machine merely
makes free of the wind
is lost to the quota

men stand on the shore
and turn their backs
on the machine

Snake time
                makes a motive
announcing the eternal
up to the minute

Breathing
            makes a hole
through which
an afternoon passes

an afternoon with
a guitar and ducks

a halo around
an aspect (mind you)
of the absolute
                the quiet chaos
a costumed mystery
a tentative circus
of phrasing energies

and

(the) music weathered
and stately so many notes
the violinist finds the quick
fuss of threads and pushes
his rage and arctic shadings
through the stubborn descant
offered and eavesdropped and
pressed into reticence
for no other reason than
what was meant was what was
needed for accents to perfect
their touch or move a
witness tongue through
an already crowded promise

Obstinate wavering
yellow yellow green yellow
invites emptiness posing
as a monstrous effort

For color bandages what's
warped in the gap anticipation
corrects and resets

Autumn
is archaic superimposed perspective

Those ingredients
make strange sorrows

you have no hands

your eyes are closed

when you speak

we use you for a calendar

Judge the transparency
but do it from the roof
the peeling echo
detached from the falling leaves
brings a voluntary to your mood
and way of thinking
I personally will take my chances in the cellar
dissipated, botanical, and full of new shadows
a universe that fell upon
the adroit ripples of casual reflection
and founded an order

A pink maniac
drags his bush of violets
his what-he-calls-it

That's health!
the Orpheus gnome can reckon

'I'll call you
on my dangerous phone'

He prances and sprawls
in his vista

His bush of violets
awakens the pastoral highlands
with a recondite symmetry only
a pink maniac could devise

It might as well
be a continent

or just an instinct
that nourishes

without the usual
labyrinth token of intuition

A bush of violets is
a safe and casual elsewhere
an excursion imitating a smile

Serious hostility carves
the vocabulary into
the future
              Complicated
long-range and forgotten

The moon rises
on claustrophobia
but the clerk only hears pianos

It was a cold night in November
and it will be
how you reply

Alone or accompanied

Red hurts black

Today's
light is chorus labor to coda
            chart of frictions
silk in cement
                the weave hardens and pulls
Gist Zeros
            the pulse that sets off thirst
            and its disguised techniques

A factory making distinctions

The great paper
and its spewn melody
disposing of the wayward but mutual

                realizes

up to the minus
means round again

crick notched to the grind

weight's direction
down and around
ticking not suspension
but angle pitted

inertia o'clock

The sunset is inkstained

wheels chasing horses

ancient coins

the walnut madhouse

to paddle the atmosphere
into altitude
clinging to the numbers
that hold back the sureties
and proven emblems
mechanics that offer no solace

debris' tattoo rising

Only you and I will ever know of it
Sneak the ordinary radiance into the spectrum
We nevertheless are black and white

However a parrot guarantees color
All that luminiferous method shocked
Elastic out of sparks and abrupt stars

Opinions cushion millions on consensus
Bright percussions honed open
Inched on stone non intoned

Hollow bone

par *para*
cowry

refuge
cone

couvade

Say as
go

Inca
tonic

Meso-
potamian

energies
stelae

shadows
root up

the face
up on

a-
long

goes
gong

The heat of thumb and forefinger
makes the page blister
Just a capacity
that blister but
the head floats free
in electric space
systems glimmer, the lengths
first counted on the fingers
of both hands until the grievous
scrutiny achieves the edges
deserved, the vague betrayed
by tenored omen nerve's dialect
in stubborn session will
talk to no one
but loud and clear
So undertaking patience
there are
the unit and
columns of situations
sought out at first
then flexed with
if I then you and
why not
what was dull is sharpened
in waiting to be used
a pen rests in
the coat pocket with
a small wad of paper
every page is covered with symbols
the code is introduced
with can I or will you
what do the curves of anxiety pursue
can I or will you
what do the spectral aspects of impulse
(vibration, horoscope, handshake, landmark, tooth)
codify
can I or will you

I say you
what are
the rights
of the accused

I say you
and you bloom
on the monitor
where it's not

enough to use
your eyes
or your hands
nickelodeon

adjustments
only make things
worse or your
shirt betrays you

I say you
and they see you
without a leg
to stand on

you can rest

Of, of—the cobwebbed genitive

48

Almanack mâché

the line points

plural to clarify

the small ebb

these words

floating in what

the hand holds

A punctured yolk is a strobed
screen spun flat, cincturing
a barrel of moons
                    burl smoke
in the astronomer's eyes
an implacable squint

Lens, moss and teeth halving
the two dimensions in matchlight

The promontory
was once an ancient spoon
above the metal towns

Poppies spun
against the sheeted limestone
migration's seed-flecked henge
a rocky spine
half fish half steamstack

False starts an acreage

Blind as a sleeve

One way
beginning with snow

Spies leap
in the dust

Carnival money
packs the bone

Final knots
threadbare
and abundant

The geography

Something more permanent and alien

Conspectus by subtraction

The heaped frieze

And no more arches

Where once ran the comfort of the narrow path

A plain of rubble

Aspect

Broken profiles

Or
the or

evasive
ovation

Or
the or

final
mountain
(inhales)

Or the
or

regard's
miracle

Or the
or

(exhales)
raggeder
apparatus

Or
or

Appropriate silence
is the broken edge

it cuts and gathers-in
Precarious integers

and depth perdu
Motionless and warm

a cadenced exception
fulfilling silence

Ragweed radio rind
the life snapped above
the watched source
ruminant breath
and nail hawks desire

To this day
the handle
the pendulum
over my head

To this day
a stone
in the wrong place
sits and floats
in the long grasses

Sits and floats
the final sense
of intimate continuity
erasing the neutral
the anatomizing
melancholy discrepancies

Memory's wedge
makes a valley
tilts the letters so
and tilts the pillar
toward the formula
that promises the angle

What measure
would I make
what measure
what re-assurance
what path

Selection
cut from stone —
an old measure

Tin to granite
graphite wrapped
in cotton

Sound cut
from the thick
night

when we built
the white
city

Map cartilage
moonlight blossom
filament in alcohol

concedes
the stop for
breath

The sense of loss

that spikes the efficiency

set it down

life's science

balanced or

octagonal

regarding corners

burned and reset thus

Sail and kite

halved by the blithe

and missing stigma

memory's division

is all the west

name the push cut

the crystal's damaged

stretch and impact wake

The sugared salt made of a name
a first word or purpose
lunging at a delegated listening
concerning the reading the face
for alarm *de legere* or delight
a flower more shape than color
vapor groom to aperture or white
prow's role explained a syllable short

Blue   oriental
      drapery

      integral

Blue   integers
      ordinal worthies

      toppled
      locked in a room

      at morning

      coming upon
      the center

Blue   formed

      the length
      of it
      a haunting
      that center

      exerting
      the mathematical phrase
      illusory
      stand
      point

original motives
superb impediment
factored out

the boundary
returns
and receives

grey horse
in blue woods
such a perfection
could only
          submit

hacked out the pure notion
makes a delicate (wait for no
consensus) oblivion (go where
you must) too often absent
from the everyday (each's each)

immunity leans
back into a web
of light
absent from

several scents
turn to taste
also once (or
more than once)
absent from

holds only
the mood with its
small notes
in the dots
absent from

apart from that
there is static
vigorous name magnet
or airflow persuasion
absent from

an anxious connived
colony in an oversimplified
wilderness whose comfortable
secrets are *absent from*

stacked up elsewhere (you
tell me whose else or which)
the encroaching errand is self-
congratulatory (motive's hammer)
remembering oblivion's terrain

fair's fair's lodged
between the i and s
of risk

and I'll tell you why

when money talks
shitheads clone

The mineral aphorism gestures
toward perfection
and props the head

a skin of sympathy when hysteria
is blue

optical spots
red circles or light scratched
through the lens
to exhibit chalk lines
from dog to horse to boat to stick

though gravity is continuous
and its mannerisms are mobilized
by sex and solitude and in many
cases paper

I know to say
I wish there
was a key to
my sleeve means
the professional
song hits a
high note but
I also know I
wish there was
a key to my
sleeve and
not up it for
the high note

The guessing budget's
a bird riot at a feeder
chirk cancels chirk
seed fractures the light
behind the wing and
nobody gets to eat
but the squirrel
who heats up the distinction
with self-congratulatory
archives of sustenance
and chatter that simplify
the noble lopes and bland
demagoguery the tempo takes to song

forensic groans
rakishly fibrillatory
clash spheres
several loins bark

sail on bistro
the morphic cupboard
and peasant chimney

prune relic perimeter
chair leaf and loaf foam
bitched stiff

ready one antler
dogs data in a glass case
muscles one facet

adieu norman gene
blossom ducts and morphine
electroshock and antihistamine

squaw balls automobile frown
monologue Sumer grille
nest makers ox of wheat

step to bald link
fuel pincers the sixteen
dictionary squid fake derby

you better listen for four
a couple of years
floating it out up front

put up or box down
nose handle assail lime
stumble trunk gravity per per

Purged of contempt they
have the peace of blame
and its politic adventure
educated in the smirk where

the parlance of history is
hectored in the long dust
and transformed in the fabulous
spectator's notebook of intuitions

where we're all a little brittle
but ignited for all that . . .
numbering the compliments and
sprucing the white feathers

over cups of kangaroo bouillon
and staging the shipshape with
shuffling ushers on the aisles—
ill-humored and impatient

for the show to begin

Today the eyes hurt
because the music is
so slow . . . cats
on the tusk . . . not
Mozart but notes on
the legends and the type
is so small the eyes
burn with the fixing *virtù*
negotiating permanence
with pure color crux
shopped by balance and
property rubbed like the eyes

Flat eye(s) piano transcriptions

that subtlety has not changed enough

flatter the sagging geranium

engineered— confected— stars

opening in the minor margins

the utterant (no word) cut

from the plural and candid

found waiting around for the best

light under the clarity that points

the way past the kitsch of metaphor

or echo-smooth singularities . . .

one, two, maybe three at a time

Good morning to what
is projected from within
after what was turned away from
took shape unprovoked by content

Good evening to what
is protected from within
after what was turned away
marched up and down and faded away

Good night to what
was protracted from without
and didn't balk to take the necessary
streaked seed or waxed rudder

Good day to what
was perfected without the illusion
after the putative halves and wholes
after the soothsaying salt turned alphabet

Blizzard chess while the patina
amounts to hardens and shines
The chisel ruminates
Catchy warmth bends at the window

Towards the restored torsion
precision is contrite
This transforms the circuits
and furnishes an undertone

Corpulent and a standard
An and and an an squatting in Sumer
marked in hard colors
Apples fall through the call for water

An arsenal of vertigo in the next
sentence

The prefix orbits
the suffix doubts
But three tales
pulled the three

First the coda
then the motive
facing the warehouse
of shared speech

One tremble pretends
one makes amends
one is a
specimen once again

Four windows times
the set of
tales assembling system
whimsy's confrontational mode

Prime
these are

the things
they do

all the assembled
stirrings

dried in summer
just as a matter

of fact
a hard sureness

pleasing to the hand
even flowers

the iodine rose
hard as a hammer

loosens the stencil
trellis from

the barn wall
and no longer able

to construct its
shadow it

falls across the dog
Ptolemaic in his path

Split sign above
the red latch
put to the edge
of smoke— envy's
hole with trapeze
dead beautiful

Thanks
for the ginger
gelding thanks
for the prolix
arabesque and your
manifesto's triangulation

Two necks and one sleeve
by antediluvian standards
quite a squint to make
the fit *e pluribus luna*
stone knot hurled back
is held in the fabric of truth

Thanks
for the pinch through space
and thanks for the room
to pump the routine artery
with the obscure vintage
the candid save for the candid

He'd never been a miscreant before
He'd always been a bleached fox
It came with the intimacy of compensation
And it demanded squander and the occasional tattoo

Out in the sun he could be inconspicuous
An angel of loneliness he had faith in himself
It was only at night that miscreant suggested
Just another stranger at the door

Humpbacked quizzical careless with the percussive
Functions that havoc signs in *mise-en-scene*
Heart sounds and glib apostrophes
Cavalier flaws pennants and biography

What suits the topography
are peninsula cities
narrow serenities
given up to waders and aureole tides
finger and thumb investigating
the green ledges and smudging
the fanning deltas purple and pearl
conversation's diffuse
transparent effluvium
heard from above
Always the mirrored choice
up but still under the hard stars
strayed instigations for craft
heard from above

Under St Awe's sill
shards of pottery
stained glass and cow shit

Under St Awe's sill
the blue grasses
of the cradling valley

Under St Awe's sill
the stone erasures not
just to be blamed on the weather

Under St Awe's sill
hymns to loaves
and lobelia

Under St Awe's sill
the hum of electrified fences
and a decimal neon confection

Under St Awe's sill
a weathered board
distracts the tongue

The black wheel stone
covered with lichen
under St Awe's sill

Solstice edges out harmony
and the light swarms
under St Awe's sill

It moves from boundary
to margin and frowns
under St Awe's sill

The charm is frail now
measured against decay
under St Awe's sill

Seasons refocus the geometry
from the column's top to the indifference
under St Awe's sill

Snow falls in a manner
similar to gossip
under St Awe's sill

The plan is
part two
like the cut
from the top
to second
cut or just
before its
start. That's
the plan.

The caper is
part three.
Making the cut.
That's before
its start or
between the
bottom of the first
cut and the top
of the second.

End of part one.

I can understand
that silence can have
its chocolate thigh
and rabbit ears
its colony of plugs
holding duress
in the drain you
put on my alien
dimensions and their
patterns of silence
but what I can't
understand is that
voiced adjunct you'd
have me share
what you call the
no I guess it's what
I call the scar structure
yes that's what
you call it when
you begin the experiment
with inks to solve the doubt
that silence persists
and speaks of the tight
and vibrating brake
when you begin with error
and end with no stasis
but the split precision

I still have another
arrangement in mind.

This does not lead
to erasure, out of necessity.

But it punctuates
the irreversible past.

That, and that alone,
is the beginning of shape.

Between the shapes
that came before there are

Climates of susceptibilities
ranging through t's and l's and b's

And through the devotional
hustle the surrogate.

It survives where crowds
are supplied with full moons

And smooth angles abstracted from
the vigorous system that blankets

Persuasion with the cryptofogolingolyrico.
Noir sur blanc.

Harp fool harp
that's the skip
you want

Harp fool harp
that's the run
you get

Even when or
even then that's
the harp fool

Harp and get
what you want
harp fool harp

When you dance
that's the good
burn lick harp

Fool harp

Limit is the distracted
consolation of exhaustion

so come no further
unless the unintentional

is restorative

Rewrite the emperors

their houses object

to the horizon

Aborigines take hostages
and resolve the tangle

the dance offered
that falls within

not the old trace
but the rhythm of the list

the tilt rational and thrifty
the lost path

between a long stain of light
and the glyphed wrack

The heating whisper
in the statue

The double's many parts

The tongue's misfortune
to esteem the ear

The betokened steppings
from urgent to chromatic

The turned and overheard
accomplishing component

Emblem conduit
Self-emphasis pieces with

The cooling spot on the thumb's
first joint

The pump works

The rhubarb grows

That's the gentry

Out of pitch

The key turns

Only in its plan

Blunderscape

And harmony

The tongue kindles

Click to order

And hum the puzzle

Rouge and magnet ache

The horn goes

The pump works

The rhubarb grows

Enough's enough only
in the head—you know
the head where the ear's
attached—there
for instance under the auspices
of an exchange of monotonies
this might be of use
or it might have to wait
or seek out a circumstance
empty of laughter
and plot a signal or series
of spells meticulous in
their capture—*summa* almost
tactile *contra* thrall

Taken together
A currency

Taken apart
A further currency

Preempted by the wish
Not to confuse or build

On a confusion but
Warn of the cosy nest

Atop the petard
Not full of eggs

But coins milled
Like gears

Differentials
Grinding out the monkey motions

Venture glosses
Twice the parade and half the brass

The rhythmic flaw
taps in the plastic box
builds the ruminative
and shapes its pace

guttural magic
pronouncing perceptions
translating skeletons
Mr Venus articulates
and feels the difference
porcelain blood is
coaxing's estate

the fictitious recognized for
the first time
completing the solipsism
thus
held up not slowed down
the first time

strategies
always
out of frame

The eventual is rarely observable
Posthumous physics (that high stepper)
Is easily eluded and the perturbed averages
Can never be stopped: a technology
Whose terms though still indistinct
Command a healthy (and humbling) record
Of accuracies when applied to what
Just might transpire if A led to B or D.

Since this is the case (and, admit it,
You're not a great dancer) where's
The pleasure in the proposition?
You're herding sheep through the wool.
And, can you believe it, the sky
Is cloudy all day. But, nevertheless,
You tell me it has its many uses.

But when we get around to picking one
Or two of these uses there's another physics
Brought to bear on this and when history
Is involved some of those earlier issues.
We walk around under the city lights
And talk about this, thinking we're keeping
The posthumous at bay when the transparent
Pulls us up short and a woman in white
Shows us how she's just smoke on the glass.

The foliage held
a shipwreck

Should we blame
it on the high winds

or the way optioned
in eureka

Argue better
the phrase that takes

less with the right
hand than the left hand gives

The flood means
rude work

to sort the trees
from the roofs

obeying the water's
faltering redundancy

The spattered arsonist
hikes his hornpipe

Finally there are
exertions practiced behind
the systematic wobble
and lurch

Smooth numbers took too
long to fill the expedient
Think dilemma and
dilemma's the burning bush

A step away from
the instructive tale
the appropriation
of polarities

A mirror swallows
the best bet
A fabric of substantiating
errors marks the interval

Next is text

100 years
before Dante
700 after

It would be
Chomei

" . . . noting
events forty years."

I'd have
help me fuse
this bomb

Pilfered
palliative
hillbreeze

Gonzaga wood
stone and lead

pigment before
character

shaped phrase
and moved

eye ear
and tongue

astrologer
and alchemist

Signorelli
Pontormo

Parmigianino
Dürer

Pico della Mirandola
for Hermes the Gatherer

We are not
approaching
the speed
of light
we are
the speed
of light
folded
inward
along a line
running
from the
spoken alphabet
to the patch
darkness fills
between the
letters

The echo
geometrizeth
Folds out
the old
opacity

The eyecho
pairs
elision parts

The echo
geometrizeth
into dimension

Protactinium

Pitchblende mote

Coiled the moon's
face fills the satellite
hole
     Cloud acoustics
tone the distance's faux pas
heard in secret combination
and seen opening like an umbrella
on the monitor

Macaronicks surge
syllable tympanum
and eyehold vectors

Screed through the plaster

Dwarf sirocco ash
and cobblestones
clod song piper to
his camel at the wall

Heat in the stem
but no flower
Valentine frigates
full of mangos

Birds tangled
in the humid leaves
flute and piano whip
yellow pearls on red flags

The dwarf sirocco ashes
the cobblestones
grape vine brimming
the garden wall

Ambient light
always to be
preferred

And light
brought
to deep
water

Blue star
making
power

Green star
making
depth

Restive spectrum
arc to ark

Lens to eye
obscures

The free man
is handcuffed to the tale

right leg extended
he hops ahead

on the left
picked out of the delirium

by the terror
of the tale

so much for the private
sense so much for

the dance
and paralysis of the myth

A is legislative to Z
    is course of action
    context to swallow
    is Z as function
    as arrived at

A holds out and Z is focal
    point of order
    not point to point
    as run at or to
    pursuit constrains

A scribing flow that attends
    to Z
    delineates or harkens
    the affectations of industry
    that pause and roll over

A march to articulate Z
    the delicate variety or
    coarse partitions
    maskings and measures derived
    confuse charm and status with

A labors and Z term
    run from surfeit to stasis
    wit to margin passes
    the quandrant framed
    as A is to Z outlawed

REM for
the savant
meanders
through
the simultaneous
level
with
the blade
dumbshine
and
cactus
grasp's
ethic
hyphens
a climax
the face
clutter
a hat
the maze
enchanted
with hair
and proud
trees
cracked
spells
sparks
in the
salve
oranges
coughing
white
locked
in the breath
carbon spines
speculate
on the thumb

The plum's
numb

Birdsong
tips the lizard

Ego
potato

Cornsilk
the dialogue

Grammar
and a shovel

Simples
with zero

Tall pages
speak of

the external
rhythms

spiked
lotus or

the shadow's
molecules

Tall pages lifted
like a spear

In camera
he counts
the points of light

In camera
barefoot
and mythical

In camera
magnified
and collapsed

First flight
in camera
motionless

A kodalith
of what the blood
does with the future

In camera
motionless sovereign
and jotting-down

Water motorized and
sleep full of explosions

No drums just passing cars
and some snow in the air

Neither depth nor
projection chases symmetry

It's illegible
or analagous

Wheat science moving
under the lion's wig

Or it's the argument's fifth
coincidence from the left

An ancestor
of the marble buffalo

Now I remember
perfectly.
But only now.
The charm
of the virtual
has been digested
by a blunt chastity.
The vacuum's eye
projects a cylinder
of light to probe
the fractured
symmetries.
I remember
perfectly. Scrutiny's
wince traces
a latitude. So only
and again just one
coheres. Then
the parting distance,
dispersal and arrangements
bound by impulse
and verb.

POTES AND POETS PRESS PUBLICATIONS

Miekal And, *Book 7, Samsara Congeries*
Bruce Andrews, *Excommunicate*
Bruce Andrews, from *Shut Up*
Todd Baron, *dark as a hat*
Dennis Barone, *Forms / Froms*
Dennis Barone, *The World / The Possibility*
Lee Bartlett, *Red Scare*
Beau Beausoleil, *in case / this way two things fell*
Steve Benson, *Two Works Based on Performance*
Charles Bernstein, *Amblyopia*
Charles Bernstein, *Conversation with Henry Hills*
Charles Bernstein, *disfrutes*
Norma Cole, *Metamorphopsia*
Clark Coolidge, *A Geology*
Cid Corman, *Essay on Poetry*
Cid Corman, *Root Song*
Tina Darragh, *Exposed Faces*
Alan Davies, *a an av es*
Alan Davies, *Mnemonotechnics*
Alan Davies, *Riot Now*
Jean Day, from *No Springs Trail*
Ray DiPalma, *New Poems*
Rachel Blau DuPlessis, *Tabula Rosa*
Johanna Drucker, from *Bookscape*
Theodore Enslin, *Case Book*
Theodore Enslin, *Meditations on Varied Grounds*
Theodore Enslin, *September's Bonfire*
Norman Fischer, *The Devices*
Steven Forth, *Calls This*
Peter Ganick, *Two Space Six*
Peter Ganick, *Met Honest Stanzas*
Carla Harryman, *Vice*
Susan Howe, *Federalist 10*
Janet Hunter, *in the absence of alphabets*
P. Inman, *backbite*

Potes & Poets Press, Inc.
181 Edgemont Avenue
Elmwood CT 06110